Chung Tai Koans

The Teaching Stories of
Grand Master Wei Chueh

Translated and Edited by
Chung Tai Chan Monastery USA

Printed in the United States of America

04 03 02 01 00 99 1 2 3 4 5 6 7 8 9

ISBN 0-9755701-0-2

Library of Congress Control Number: 2004108288

Spiritual Teacher and Honorary Publisher
Grand Master Wei Chueh

Supervising Editors and Publisher
Venerable Abbot JianLiao
Venerable Master JianYing

Managing Editor and Art Director
Barbara Simpson, www.designbright.com

Contributing Editors and Translators
Buang Ann Tay
Kristy Yao
Brian J. Nichols

 Cover and illustration artwork
Jamie Zhang, www.JamieZhang.com

Editorial and production assistance
Samantha Simpson
Sally Strong

Four Tenets of Chung Tai

To our elders be respectful.
To our juniors be kind.
With all humanity be harmonious.
In all endeavors be true.

Grand Master Wei Chueh

Grand Master Wei Chueh and Chung Tai Chan Monastery

From an ascetic to a great Chan master.

From hosting seven day Chan retreats for only twenty to hosting them for thousands of people today.

From a sangha of just four ordained and three hundred lay disciples in 1987, to the sangha of more than one thousand ordained and hundreds of thousands of lay disciples today.

Grand Master Wei Chueh has ardently brought the teaching of Chan (Zen) to people around the world. A holder of the Linji (Rinzai) lineage, the teaching of the Grand Master is straightforward, as it directly points to the mind in ways that are congruent with the students' aptitudes. His teaching is flexible yet on the mark; a word, a gesture, or even silence inspires students. As the founder of Chung Tai Chan Monastery, the Grand Master has tirelessly led seven-day meditation retreats and given Dharma lectures in Taiwan and abroad over the past decades to help people cope with their pressures and restless minds so prevalent in the fast-paced life of today.

The story of the Grand Master and Chung Tai began in the early 1970s when Grand Master Wei Chueh began his secluded, austere practice in the Yang Ming Mountains near the Wanli area of Taipei County, Taiwan.

i

He lived in extremely poor and primitive conditions, but practiced the Dharma with joy. Over the next twelve years, he was gradually discovered by people passing by, and soon he had many followers. He then established Ling Chuan Monastery, where his disciples could gather to study Buddhism and practice Chan. In Ling Chuan Monastery, the Grand Master gave lectures and conducted many seven day Chan meditation retreats. People were attracted by his straightforward teaching and Chan wisdom. Soon he was known as the master who revived the Chan tradition in Taiwan, and Ling Chuan Monastery was no longer big enough to accommodate all the people who wanted to practice there.

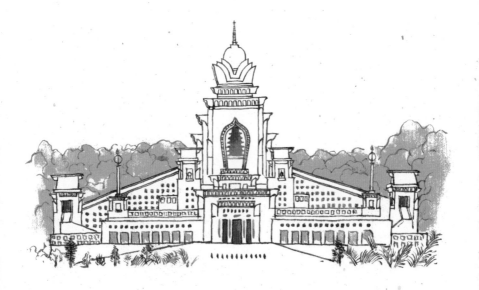

Chung Tai Chan Monastery, Nantou, Taiwan

Upon the request of all disciples, Grand Master Wei Chueh then founded Chung Tai Chan Monastery in Puli in central Taiwan in 1987. After more than a decade of careful planning and construction, the new Chung Tai Chan Monastery was finally inaugurated on the first day of September, 2001. As one of the largest Buddhist monasteries and sanghas in the world, Chung Tai integrates the teachings of sudden enlightenment and gradual cultivation, with the altruistic and ascetic practices of Buddhist traditions. Its architecture embodies modern-day technology and artistry, serving to unify religions, academic research, cultures, and the arts of the East and the West. The establishment of Chung Tai is also a demonstration of the Grand Master's devotion to encouraging an era of global religious dialogue.

Under the guidance of the Grand Master, Chung Tai emphasizes three aspects in practicing the teachings of the Buddha: Scriptural studies, deeds of beneficence, and meditation. Scriptural studies lead to right views, deeds of beneficence lead to accumulated merits and resources, and meditation facilitates seeing the true nature. With diligent practice of these three aspects, one integrates theoretical study with meditative insight, as well as the altruistic practice of the Bodhisattva path.

To further integrate Chan teachings into daily life, Grand Master Wei Chueh emphasizes the importance of upayas (skillful means) and specifically enlightens all practitioners with the Four Tenets of Chung Tai:

To our elders be respectful.
To our juniors be kind.
With all humanity be harmonious.
In all endeavors be true.

The Grand Master once explained, "With respect, we eradicate arrogance; with compassion, we extinguish anger and hatred; with harmony, we eliminate violence; with truth and sincerity, we eradicate deceit." He further asserted, "To attain Middle Way Reality, we observe the Four Tenets of Chung Tai."

Under the guidance of Grand Master Wei Chueh and with his unified and practical approach, Chung Tai now has established more than eighty meditation centers and branches in Taiwan and abroad in the hope of bringing a safer and more peaceful world for all generations to come.

Contents

Foreword

The word *koan* originated from the Chinese word *gong-an*, which was an official legal document that served as a ruling standard in the public courts of ancient China. In Chan or Zen Buddhism, the koan has historically recorded the classic exemplary teachings of the Chan patriarchs.

With the help of these inspiring and enlightening masters' teachings, contemporary practitioners can learn, discover, and realize the true meaning of Chan Buddhism. Using koans, Chan masters throughout history have shown the way for seekers to focus the mind in specific ways and learn self-reflection, to let go of attachments and to finally realize their own true nature. Reading and exploring the koans with the understanding of not departing from one's true mind will bring the most benefit to practitioners.

Chung Tai Koans is a collection of the teaching stories of Grand Master Wei Chueh, who is the founding abbot of Chung Tai Chan Monastery in Taiwan. In these stories, with his profound wisdom and compassion, along with his solid and deep understanding of Chan, Grand Master Wei Chueh transforms the ancient wisdom of Chan into present-day activities and provides precious opportunities for all practitioners to explore their true, inner life.

Each of the Chung Tai koans in this book has its own profound implications and represents a manifestation of our intrinsic Buddha nature. When reading the koans, reflect carefully, meditate, and delve deeply for the significance and meaning. In so doing, it will definitely bring great benefits to all practitioners and ultimately lead to enlightening the mind and seeing one's true nature.

Realizing the profound teachings of Chan will elevate practitioners to an inspired and illuminated life path. It is our desire and the sole purpose of translating and publishing these koans that each and every reader will awaken to the radiance behind the clouds and walk the bright path every moment of every day.

Chung Tai Chan Monastery USA

Chung Tai Koans

Upon Reflection

A certain monk had the habit of wearing a sweater over his shoulders with the sleeves tied in front. One day the Grand Master was observed walking around the monastery with a sweater wrapped around his shoulders in exactly the same manner. Upon seeing the Grand Master's unusual appearance, the monks began discussing his behavior with each other and wondered, "Why is the Grand Master dressed like this? That is so strange!"

In the middle of this chattering, the monk walked in and saw the Grand Master. Smiling to himself, the monk never wore a sweater this way again.

Pick Up the Beat

Once during a morning service, the monks were all chanting with great concentration. Unexpectedly, the Grand Master walked in with his hands folded behind his back. His eyes were cast down looking back and forth across the ground. The monk on duty hurried over and asked, "Grand Master, are you searching for something?" The Grand Master replied, "The beats! Haven't you seen them? The beats are all over the floor! Go fetch a broom and sweep them up!"

After the service, the monks who were responsible for playing the ritual instruments and leading the ceremony knelt in front of the Buddha statue in repentance.

Snakes and Cultivation

Located in the Yang Ming Mountains, Ling Chuan Monastery occasionally receives visits from snakes. One day the sight of a big boa startled some nuns, who screamed out in surprise. Witnessing their reaction, the Grand Master said to them, "This is not a courteous way to treat another sentient being that comes to cultivate its Bodhi mind. You should get along in harmony."

On another day, a small snake appeared in the Chan Hall. It was moving in a rectangular pattern, similar to the monks' walking meditation. The attendant monk of the hall bent down to give the snake the Three Refuges, and then asked it to leave. The snake persisted with its own "walking meditation" and showed no sign of leaving. Suddenly, the Grand Master walked in and said, "Go." The snake went away immediately.

Such is the difference in authority and insight intrinsic to cultivation.

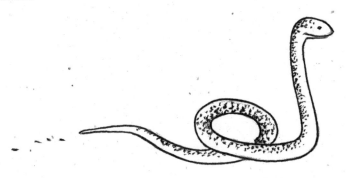

Dharma Steps

A newly ordained monk had heard that a Chan Master lives the Dharma with every word he speaks and every action he takes. Considering this, he decided to pay particular attention to how the Grand Master put on his shoes.

The first time he observed the Grand Master upon leaving the Grand Hall, the Master sat down to put on his shoes. When he observed the Master for the second time, he was leaving his office. This time, the Master put one hand against the wall and put on his shoes with the other hand. On the third occasion, the monk noticed that the Grand Master was leaving the Chan Hall. This time he slipped on his shoes by actually walking in them for a short distance.

One day shortly after he made these observations, the monk was reading the *Diamond Sutra*. As he read these words from the beginning passage, "Putting on his robe and holding the bowl, the Buddha entered Sravasti on foot to ask for alms food," the monk had a sudden realization: Observe how the Grand Master uses his mind while he puts on his shoes.

Sitting Through the Night

A very dedicated and diligent nun desired to practice the method of meditation called sitting through the night. She inquired of the Grand Master how she might achieve this goal.

The Grand Master responded, "Not to give rise to a single thought is the meditation of sitting through the night."

Unmoving Mind

At the Ling Chuan Monastery during a staff meeting, the Grand Master harshly pointed out that the monks' chanting was unacceptable. He called on the chef monk, "Tell me what the reason is: Is it because you didn't cook enough food so that everyone had to chant with an empty stomach?" Obediently, the chef monk stood up with his palms together and said "Yes, Grand Master."

As the meeting continued, the Grand Master learned that construction was behind schedule. He called on the chef monk again, "Did you forget to prepare snacks for the monks who were working hard at the construction site? Is that why we are behind schedule?" The chef monk replied respectfully, "Yes, Grand Master."

Throughout the meeting the chef monk repeatedly stood up in response to the Grand Master's severe questioning, each time calmly answering only with "Yes, Grand Master."

Too Tired

One day a monk asked, "Grand Master, I am doing many chores at the same time. Is there one chore I can do without?" The Grand Master asked, "Why?" The monk responded, "I am very tired."

The Grand Master remarked, "I am very tired, too."

The monk, "…"

What Time Is It Now?

In the early days of the construction of Ling Chuan Monastery, the Grand Master always led his disciples to do physical labor at the construction site until at least midnight. One night, a monk inquired of the Grand Master, "Master, it is already late. Is it time to take a break?" The Grand Master asked, "What time is it now?" "It is one hour before midnight," the monk replied. The Grand Master turned to him and said, "Oh! It is just now daytime in the United States."

The monk paused for a while and then continued to complete the work with the Grand Master until one o'clock in the morning. When they were finished for the night, he realized that he did not feel sleepy at all. Suddenly, the words of the Grand Master came to him, "Sleeping is also a wandering thought!"

Birthday Party

A lay disciple wanted to organize a birthday celebration for the Grand Master. He asked the Grand Master for the date of his birth; the Grand Master smiled but did not answer. The lay disciple did not comprehend, so he asked again.

The Grand Master said, "Where there is birth, there is death. Monks do not celebrate birthdays."

Not You

A monk in an important executive position at the monastery was facing difficult personnel issues with much exasperation daily. As his concerns grew, he turned to the Grand Master and expressed his frustration.

The Grand Master replied, "Others can have worries, but not you!" Immediately, the monk's concerns disappeared without a trace.

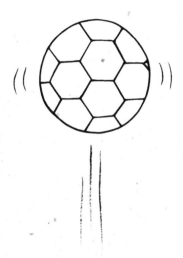

Bouncing Ball

One of the monks was troubled with his wandering thoughts. Not knowing how to deal with them, he had no peace and asked the Grand Master what to do.

The Grand Master said, "Thoughts come, and thoughts go. Just ignore them. Like a bouncing ball, if you don't hit it, it won't bounce."

Chung Tai Koans

Hammer Dharma

A novice monk had been laboring for quite some time. Not knowing the ways of cultivation, he was weary of the work. When he met the Grand Master one day, he knelt down and asked respectfully, "Grand Master, what is the Buddha Dharma?"

The Grand Master picked up a hammer and a chisel, and he struck the wall saying, "This is Buddha Dharma."

Assuming Responsibility

Once after a meeting was completed, a monk happened to remain in the conference room. The Grand Master, who was also in the room meditating, suddenly reproached the monk.

The monk first thought to himself, "I did not make those mistakes. Why am I being accused?" But then he immediately turned to another unspoken thought, "Grand Master, I am willing to learn to bear responsibility!"

Immediately he looked up to see the glimmer of a smile radiating from the Grand Master.

Practice Benefits

Not long ago, a new monk was ordained. One day, he saw the Grand Master coming back to the monastery. When the Grand Master saw the novice monk, the Grand Master sat down with him and seemed to be very tired.

The novice monk was feeling very compassionate. He inquired of the Grand Master with care, "Master, are you tired?"

The Grand Master replied immediately, "When the body is weary, take a rest; when the mind wanders away, bring it back. Practicing the Dharma is our own matter, helping sentient beings is our duty."

Old Habits

A nun proudly told the Grand Master, "I no longer get angry when responding to unpleasant events, unlike that certain other bhiksuni!" The Grand Master smiled but said nothing.

Shortly afterwards, the nun made a request to the Grand Master but was denied. She suddenly stomped her foot and exclaimed, "Grand Master, you are always like this!" The Grand Master pointed at her and asked, "What manner of behavior is this?"

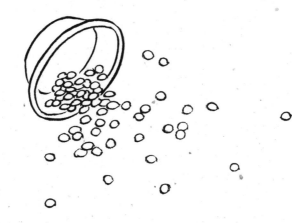

Spilled Beans

One night the disciples were sifting through the beans together when someone accidentally tipped over the pan. As everyone focused on picking up the spilled beans, the Grand Master suddenly turned off the light and asked, "Where is it?"

False or Not?

A monk who served at a meditation center thought to himself, "Since every worldly thing is like a dream or mirage, it seems there is no difference whether I work diligently or not."

One day the Grand Master came to the center. He saw on a table an artificial flower which was full of crystal clear artificial water drops. Pointing to the flower, the Grand Master asked, "Are the water drops authentic or artificial?" The monk responded, "Artificial."

A minute later, the Grand Master asked again, "Are the water drops real or not?" Puzzled, the monk emphasized, "Yes, Grand Master. They are ar-ti-fi-cial." A minute later, the Grand Master asked again, "Are the water drops real or fake?" Astonished, the monk replied, "Grand Master, the water drops are fake ones." The Grand Master smiled and said, "Faked like real."

Afterwards, the monk thought of this incident for a long time and suddenly came to a realization, "Although every worldly phenomenon is like an illusion, a Bodhisattva still diligently pursues seemingly illusory activities truthfully with integrity."

Chung Tai Koans

Sharing Bitterness*

In the early days of Ling Chuan Monastery, there was a lay disciple who sincerely offered a bundle of bitter tea to the monastery. All of the monks and nuns at the monastery did not like to drink the bitter tea and always put it aside rather than drink it.

Observing this the Grand Master said, "Since you do not like to drink bitter tea, let me take it for you." Upon hearing this, all of the disciples heartily felt the compassion of the Grand Master. They understood the dedication and seriousness of his vow to remove the suffering and bring ultimate bliss to all sentient beings.

Never Too Old

A monk who served as an abbot complained, "Grand Master, I am getting older, and I wish to rest. I don't want to be the abbot." Surprised, the Grand Master asked, "How old are you?" The monk replied, "Fifty years old."

The Grand Master then reacted with, "I am already in my seventies!" He added, "Practicing the Dharma and helping sentient beings is not dependent on a certain age. It is not about our own personal desires but only about helping all sentient beings to be liberated from suffering. That is our responsibility."

---

*In Chinese, the word "bitterness" also means "suffering."

What Illusory Thoughts?

A newly ordained monk often thought of his family. One night he missed his father so much that he began to worry about him. The next morning when he opened his door, the Grand Master was standing there with a harsh question, "Why such an illusory thought!"

Bewildered, the new monk responded with a question, "What illusory thoughts?" He then respectfully explained to the Grand Master, "Last night I only thought of my family." The Grand Master immediately responded, "That is the illusory thought."

Suddenly the young monk understood, "The moment that one raises a conceptual thought implies that one has departed from the truth. Every conceptual thought is an illusory thought. A Buddhist monk's duty is to practice diligently to achieve awakening, and to do so is a sign of great respect to his parents." Upon this realization, he immediately ceased his illusory thoughts.

Trees in Chung Tai

Just beginning his studies at the Buddhist institute, one monk worked very hard but still felt he did not understand the fundamental Buddhist teachings and needed direction.

By accident one day, he encountered the Grand Master who was taking a walk. Excited, he rushed in front of the Grand Master sincerely putting his palms together, and asked, "Grand Master, I have worked very hard to understand the fundamental teachings but still do not feel confident. What should I do?"

The Grand Master responded, "Do you know how many trees there are in Chung Tai?"

Babysitter

D ue to a heavy load of instructing novice nuns, the nun in charge applied to the Grand Master to request another nun to assist her. The Grand Master asked, "How many novice nuns are there right now?" The nun responded, "Fourteen." The Grand Master said, "Is it not true that ordinary schools outside the monastery normally have fifty students in one class?" The nun responded, "But that is different! They only need to take care of their students for eight hours a day, but I have to be with them for all 24 hours a day."

The Grand Master said, "I have over one thousand ordained disciples. What should I do?" The nun put her palms together in silence, with a new resolve to accept the responsibility.

The True Meaning
of Non-Withdrawing

A monk who had been the abbot at a meditation center for many years had experienced countless difficulties. He began to feel mentally and physically frustrated in teaching the Dharma and practicing the path of a Bodhisattva. One day, the Grand Master came to the center for a meal. Although it was way past meal time when the Grand Master arrived, the abbot observed that he was calm and centered. The Grand Master had been on the road for days and given dharma lectures one after another, and yet he displayed not a single trace of impatience.

The abbot inquired, "Grand Master, the social climate for teaching the Dharma gets worse and worse. Why do you still construct monasteries and meditation centers? Although determined to help all sentient beings to learn the Dharma, why does your mind not withdraw for even a single moment?"

The Grand Master serenely answered, "When times are troubled and conditions are becoming worse, if your mind remains calm and tranquil, this is the true meaning of non-withdrawing."

Learning of Non-Learning

A frustrated monk asked the Grand Master, "Master, it seems to take forever to learn all the required things. What can I do?" The Grand Master responded, "When you understand the learning of non-learning, then you have completed the learning, perfect and complete!" He continued, "Unending learning is based on compassion. Learning is none other than concentration, effort, and accumulation of merits. Besides learning, we also need to know the principle of non-learning."

Now You Can Come Over

One day the Grand Master led a handful of monks and lay-disciples to survey the construction of the new Chung Tai Chan Monastery. They suddenly came upon a section of muddy path, and while everyone was worrying about how to pass it, they looked over to see the Grand Master gracefully and skillful hopping through the muddy path. As if without effort, he picked up two rocks and placed them in the middle of the path. He then said to them, "Now you can come over."

Tofu Lesson

One day at lunch the disciples found that the meal consisted of dishes all made of tofu: steamed tofu, boiled tofu, fried tofu, and tofu soup. They questioned the chef monk, "Why is there nothing but tofu on the table?" The chef monk retorted, "Who was craving tofu recently?" Four or five disciples conceded that they had been thinking of tofu just the day before.

The chef monk responded, "The Grand Master often cautions us about not letting our thoughts wander carelessly at the monastery. All day long the temple has been receiving offerings of tofu!"

Polishing Pebbles

M any years ago, the Grand Master observed at his feet the clear, rippling waters of the creek at the Ling Chuan Monastery, and he said to the monk who was standing beside him, "In the years to come, my disciples will all look very much like the perfectly round pebbles in this rushing creek."

In the ensuing years, many disciples have come to be students of the Grand Master. All of his disciples have indeed grown round in the continuous flow of the Grand Master's Dharma teachings as well as from the grinding and polishing interactions of each other's contradictions and inspirations.

Earthworm Puzzle

I n the early days of Ling Chuan Monastery the monks were working on its expansion. One day while digging ground, an earthworm chopped in two was discovered, and each half was wriggling by itself.

The Grand Master observed this discovery and asked, "In which end resides the Buddha nature?"

All were silent.

Dissolving Karmic Hindrances

During a meditation session at the Ling Chuan Monastery, the Grand Master came to personally observe the session. During his observation period, the Grand Master applied the awakening staff* on almost all of the disciples with the exception of one monk. The monk wondered to himself, "To be hit isn't that bad; it helps to dissolve one's karmic hindrances."

At that very moment, the Grand Master appeared before him and bent forward slightly. Looking directly at the monk, he remarked, "One should dissolve one's hindrances on one's own."

Foreman of the Foreman

One day the Grand Master directed a monk, "Ask a foreman to complete this project."

The monk responded, "Grand Master, you have already handed this project to the foreman, haven't you?"

The Grand Master replied, "You are the foreman of the foreman."

*An instrument used to ensure attention and discipline in the Chan hall.

Chung Tai Koans

One's Own Children

A monk felt he had encountered a setback, and he told the Grand Master, "It is really difficult to teach the Dharma to sentient beings sometimes. Often they are not only stubborn, but they also criticize the Dharma and insult the Sangha. That's really frustrating!"

The Grand Master answered, "Buddhas and Bodhisattvas treat sentient beings like their own children such that when their child makes a mistake, they only hope that the child will learn from it and correct it. How can a parent be angry with their child?"

The monk was really touched and inspired upon hearing this.

Take Leave of Life and Death

A monk, who wished to visit his family, asked the Grand Master for a leave.

The Grand Master said, "That's okay, but ask for it from King Yama who is in charge of death." The monk was suddenly illuminated and found inspiration at that moment.

Whoever Comes Is the Guest

One day, the Grand Master walked into the receptionist office and asked, "What kind of receptionist are you? You are not even aware that someone has come in." The receptionist monk was puzzled, "That's strange. Has someone sneaked into the monastery?"

The Grand Master said, "A chicken has gone into the Yun-Lai Hall. Don't you know that?" The monk thought, "But he didn't come here to check in."

Hard-to-Find Opportunities

There was a certain taciturn and introspective monk who always felt uneasy when facing the public. He was afraid he may not be able to deal with different people in various circumstances.

One day the monk appealed to the Grand Master, "I am afraid to face the public. What should I do?" The Grand Master responded, "Without sentient beings it is impossible to fulfill the merits of Bodhisattvas. When facing anxieties brought about by others, we should view this circumstance as a hard-to-find-opportunity, and think: They are all facilitating my practice."

Goldthread* Gets Rid of Poison

Whenever he completed a task assigned to him by the Grand Master, one particular monk was always anticipating and expecting the Master's recognition and praise. Once when he had completed a task and was expecting praise, the Grand Master suddenly turned to him and said, "Don't think of eating candies every day. You should eat more goldthread to get rid of the poison in your body."

*A bitter Chinese medicine.

Steamed Buns

A disciple took the Grand Master to the airport, but since his schedule was too hectic, the Grand Master had no time to eat the breakfast prepared by the chef monk much earlier. When they had arrived at the airport a short while later, the Grand Master was about to board the plane. Meanwhile, the disciple was worrying about what to do with the prepared breakfast and thinking to himself, "I usually don't eat steamed buns, but today I probably need to eat all of them?"

At this very moment, the Grand Master came over and asked, "Where are the prepared steamed buns?" The Grand Master then finished up all the buns and vegetables, too! The chagrined disciple stood by in silence.

Wandering Thoughts

One day a certain monk drove the Grand Master outside the monastery. When they passed by the Taipei World Trade Center, the monk thought, "Master must not know of the Taipei World Trade Center. Let me seize this opportunity to introduce it to him."

He then said, "Grand Master, This is the Taipei World Trade Center." Unexpectedly, the Grand Master reminded him sternly, "Just drive when you are driving. Why such wandering thoughts?"

Formless Sentient Beings*

A lay disciple asked the Grand Master, "Master, when formless sentient beings come to haunt us, what should we do?"

The Grand Master replied, "Insofar as they are formless, why should you be attached to them?"

*A Chinese euphemistic term for ghosts.

The Secret of Master's Shoes

A few visitors were led by the Grand Master to visit the Shakya Garden that was still under construction. Since it was just after a rainfall, the pathway was very muddy. Following closely behind the Grand Master, the visitors felt ashamed for dirtying the brick they stepped on. To their surprise, the visitors noticed that the Grand Master did not leave a single trace of mud where he walked on the path.

In a tea break later, the visitors revealed their surprise publicly. From this moment on, the story with this revelation that "The Master's shoes don't get dirty" was spread with great amusement.

After another rainy day, the Grand Master went to the Shakya Garden again. On his way back when he passed by the Kwan Yin Hall, he suddenly stopped the driver. He got out of the car and went near the drain. In front of the public, he removed his shoes and holding them in his hand, he hit them hard up against the side of the drain where the mud fell off of the shoes. After he had completed this process on both of his shoes, he put them back on, got back in the car and "Slam!" After closing the door, the driver drove away.

Stop Breathing?

A certain monk was unable to fully comprehend and integrate the Mahayana and Hinayana disciplinary codes, and was very puzzled. One day, he asked the Grand Master, "When constructing a monastery, we need to weed the grass, and this will hurt many sentient beings like the insects and ants. Is this breaking the precept of non-killing?"

The Grand Master asked him in return, "Every single breath we take hurts many microbes too. Will you not breathe anymore? There are a lot of tiny beings among our individual hairs. Will you not wash your hair anymore?"

The Master continued, "When building monasteries, through the dedication of merits we bring unlimited merits to countless sentient beings."

In the Proper Place

The Grand Master led some visitors on a tour of the Chung Tai Buddhist Institute for the nuns. When he passed by the laundry room, he noticed that the washing machine was not placed properly, and the mop was slightly tilted. He immediately returned the machine and mop to the correct positions, and instructed, "Everything must be in the proper place."

Public Offering

The fruit tree in front of the conference room was bountiful and bore lots of star fruits. Unfortunately, the fruits fell all over the ground attracting countless ants to the area. Someone had an idea to preserve the fruits and offer them to the public but then hesitated because this might be against the precept of non-stealing. Thus he sought the advice of the Grand Master.

The Grand Master responded, "For the fruits growing on the trees in the monastery, do not pluck them. They are very fragrant, which enhances the air, and moreover, many ghosts and deities especially like this fragrant smell. When the star fruits have grown yellowish and the spectators see them, it will bring them joy, and that is indeed an offering to the public!"

Nothing Too Difficult

A sixty-year-old monk did not have a very big vocabulary; and after he became a monk he asked the Grand Master, "Master, which sutra should I recite?" The Grand Master answered, "The *Heart Sutra*." "But, I would like to recite the *Diamond Sutra*," the old monk interjected. The Grand Master smiled and said nothing.

Every day, the old monk opened the sutra, put his palms together and recited loudly and sincerely, "Namo Shakyamuni Buddha." After reciting the Buddha's name three times, he would stare intently at the sutra and read mindfully, "Thus-have-thus have-I-I heard-thus have I heard..." Then it was followed by silence for a while...the old monk dropped his head, and fell asleep.

Suddenly, the three phrases "Namo Shakyamuni Buddha" broke the silence again, the old monk regained his spirit and learned to read with great effort, "Thus-have-I-heard...At-one-time..." After a pause, the old monk again fell asleep.

On another occasion, the Grand Master gave instructions to a gathering, "There is someone, I have asked him to recite the *Heart Sutra*, but he still wants to recite the *Diamond Sutra*." When he heard this, the old monk was more determined and started to ask around, "How do you read this word? Oh! N-u... Ah! What about this one..." After one year, the old monk had recited the *Diamond Sutra* three thousand times.

Hot or Not?

On a very hot afternoon, together with a few lay disciples, the Grand Master was taking a walk. All of the lay disciples were feeling extremely hot and uneasy in addition to sweating all over. But looking at the Grand Master who had walked ahead, they observed he appeared very calm and tranquil with not a drop of sweat to be seen on him. They were compelled to ask, "Master, are you not feeling hot?"

"Hot? Just don't resonate with it."

Chung Tai Koans

Breakfast with the Grand Master

Early one morning, an upset lay disciple came to the Ling Chuan Monastery, intending to complain to the Grand Master about his difficulties. After waiting for a while, the Grand Master returned to the monastery in a car. When the disciple saw the Grand Master, he was very surprised by his appearance. The Grand Master seemed to be very weak with untidy clothes and a disorderly monk bag. The man hastily asked what had happened to the Master. The Master responded weakly, "I've caught a cold and feel uncomfortable."

At this very moment the chef monk asked the Grand Master whether or not he wanted to have breakfast, and the Master responded, "I don't feel like eating." Concerned, the lay disciple persuaded the Grand Master, "Master, even if you are sick you still need to eat. When your body has energy you will recover easily. We can eat together, and I will eat as much as you do!" After the breakfast was served, the Master finished the rice and vegetables in front of him in a very short while. (He did not look like a sick person at all.)

Seeing the Master had finished his meal, the disciple hurriedly ate his breakfast. But the Grand Master waited for a while longer until he could not take any more food. Observing the still unfinished dishes, the Grand Master smiled compassionately and asked to have the dishes cleaned. The lay disciple then asked the Grand Master to get some rest.

The lay disciple finally left the monastery. He had completely forgotten his intention to complain to the Master.

The Master's Lunch

A lay disciple became the personal attendant of Grand Master. One day after the Grand Master had finished his lunch, the new personal attendant brought in yet another large plate of food. The Master advised him seriously, "I am already full."

But the disciple said boldly, "Grand Master, the disciples offer this food to you with good intentions and veneration. If you do not eat it, they will scold me." When the Master heard this, he said, "Leave the food here, and go take a break."

The disciple thought to himself, "Grand Master must be really full and is unable to eat any more food."

Nevertheless when he later came back to collect the plate and utensils, he was surprised to find a plate completely clean of food on the table. He was really chagrined and embarrassed, and thought, "To help me avoid a scolding and even though he was stuffed, the Grand Master finished all the food."

Cabbage Chant

The Grand Master forbade the chef monk to purchase processed foods for the monastery. The chef monk was only allowed to use processed foods if they were brought by lay disciples as offerings. One day the chef monk realized that there had been nothing but cabbage, radish, and tofu in the pantry for days. Because he was running out of ideas for new dishes to cook, he turned to the Grand Master for advice.

In response, the Grand Master said, "Don't we chant the same sutra every morning?"

The Dharma of Walking

There was a man who had practiced the Dharma for over ten years before he became a monk. For six consecutive years, he had organized national activities that gave offerings to the monks, and he was an important leader for the Buddhist community in the south of Taiwan. Once somebody asked him, "Why didn't you become a monk before since you practiced for so long? Why was it that after you met the Grand Master one time, you immediately decided to be a monk?" The monk replied, "Just learning how the Grand Master walks will already take a whole lifetime."

Strike the Wooden Plank* on Time

Before becoming a monk, a certain disciple worried that he would not be able to wake up on time to attend the morning service at 4:30 am.

He appealed to the Grand Master, "Master, if I can't get up, may I be excused from the morning service?" The Grand Master replied, "That's fine."

After he became a monk, the chore assigned to him was striking the wooden plank at 3:45 am.

---

*In the monastery, the sound of hitting the wooden plank is a signal to wake up, to take a rest, and to gather.

Strict Master, Great Disciple

In the early days of constructing the Ling Chuan Monastery, there was much hard work to be done. The eldest disciple of the Grand Master was seen tirelessly transporting the 50~60 kilograms of cement bundles; he and all of the other monks were seen continuously working hard and sweating profusely.

Once, the Grand Master suddenly turned to the eldest disciple and started to reproach him, "How many times have I told you to prepare snacks for people who are out here working? Why didn't you prepare any snacks?" The monk joined his palms together and said respectfully, "Yes, Grand Master."

On another occasion when everyone went out to transport stones, a nun who was not strong enough to move a big stone accidentally dropped it into the mountain gorge, and it was moving directly towards the Grand Master. The Grand Master jumped aside to avoid the stone and pointed his finger at the eldest disciple, chiding him, "That's all your fault." The monk joined his palms together, and said respectfully, "Yes, Grand Master."

When a monk said something inappropriate, the Grand Master chided the eldest disciple, "That's all your fault." When yet another monk made a mistake, the Grand Master would scold the eldest disciple, "It's again all your fault." The eldest disciple of the Grand Master would always join his palms together and respond respectfully, "Yes, Grand Master."

Chung Tai Koans

Unity Is Strength

When constructing the Ling Chuan Monastery, there was not enough funding to make payroll and so it was difficult to hire workers. Early in the morning, the monks silently gathered and decided to go out and gather alms to raise funds. When the Grand Master found out about it, he said compassionately, "There is no need to do this. It will be okay."

But late in the night while everyone else was sleeping, there was one person working silently at the construction site. When one of the monks went out to check, he found that it was the Grand Master.

On another day, a monk found that the Grand Master was moving stones to a corner. He hurried over to help him and said, "Grand Master, please just let us do that." Without even lifting his head, the Grand Master said, "You do yours, and I will do mine."

When the workers were through and left for the day, the Grand Master and all the disciples continued to work at night. From flat ground, they laid stones, built walls with bricks, and put tiles on the roofs. They worked diligently. One by one, Chan Hall, Dining Hall, Yun-Lai Hall, as well as other buildings, all gradually stood tall from the ground.

Convincing Evidence

There once was a chauffeur whose boss was a big businessman. After his boss took refuge in the Three Jewels with the Grand Master, the driver was frequently called upon to drive his boss to the monastery either early in the morning or late in the evening. Soon he became very bitter about this situation.

Therefore every time his boss spoke to the Grand Master, he would sit by his side and silently curse the Grand Master with inflammatory remarks like, "Stop lying to people, you pretentious monk!"

But soon he noticed that every time he raised a thought to condemn the Grand Master, the Grand Master would just so happen to turn his head and give him a glance. After a few times, he found that the same situation always recurred. The chauffeur then was sincerely convinced and became a devout disciple of the Grand Master. ·

Who Is the Master?

One day, the abbot at a meditation center received a call, "Hello, I am Shifu." The abbot felt strange, why did this old man call himself 'Shifu'? He then answered, "How can you be Shifu? I am the Shifu here!" The old man said, "Oh? Yes! Shifu, Amitofo!" and hung up.

Shortly thereafter, the abbot received another call. It was from the personal attendant of the Grand Master, "Hello! Venerable, did Shifu call you a moment ago?"

The abbot was stunned into silence.

A Stroke on the Head*

A monk was questioning the Grand Master, "I heard that when we take the ten great vows of Bodhisattva Samantabhadra, this will invoke him to arrive with his elephant carriage and give the ones who take the vows a stroke on the head."

The Grand Master responded, "Only kids need others to stroke their heads, not adults. Do you want me to stroke your head?"

*Buddhas and Bodhisattvas stroke their disciples' heads with their hands to ordain a title or to show their support and concern.

Letting Go

Most designers usually want to establish their own certain style and preferences. At Chung Tai, the Grand Master always teaches the disciples the primary importance of letting go.

In every design project, the designated monk would create a variety of designs and ask for the Grand Master's opinion. Invariably, the designers would put the designs they deem to be unsatisfactory at the bottom and most unobvious place. Ironically, the Master almost always picks one of the most unexpected designs. Surprisingly, an unforeseen paradox and perfect result is always revealed at the project's conclusion.

When the designers are no longer attached to their own views, the Grand Master will say, "Good! This is a nice way to do it! Let's follow this idea."

What It Means to Serve

B ecause of his low blood pressure, one of the monks was unable to join the morning and evening services, and this made him feel uncomfortable. He came to the Grand Master's office and asked, "Grand Master, since I am not able to join the morning and evening services, what should I do?" The Grand Master said indifferently, "Unable to attend the morning and evening services, that's fine."

Questioning this information, the monk interjected, "But it is the duty of a monk to attend the morning and evening services." The Grand Master responded, "Working earnestly is equivalent to attending services, and working with a mind undisturbed is the same as attending the services." Upon hearing this, the monk was greatly inspired.

The Duty of Monks and Nuns

A monk was injured accidentally in the preparation of a Dharma ceremony. The Grand Master wanted him to take a rest and treat his injury, but he could not forget about the ceremony and stubbornly insisted on continuing his work.

The monk asked, "Isn't helping sentient beings the duty of a monk?"

The Grand Master replied, "Holding on to the right thought at every moment is the duty of monks and nuns."

There Is Still a Little...

In a very limited time, a few monks produced a specially issued booklet entitled, "Chung Tai Picks up a Flower." It was well received by the public who requested a second printing of the booklet. The chief editor monk was overjoyed when he talked to the Grand Master, "The booklet is in great demand, and we only have a little stock left. Do we need to print more?" Thinking he would be praised, the chief editor monk instead heard the Grand Master say, "Don't print it anymore! The editing is not good. Look, why use this picture in this place? When we work on something, we need to do it well..."

Later, when the chief editor monk met the monk who was in charge of purchasing, the distressed editor reported that the Grand Master said not to print the booklet anymore.

The monk who was in charge of purchasing answered with astonishment, "The Grand Master just told me to order another 50,000 copies."

Don't Wait Until Next life

A monk who had encountered an obstacle in his practice became doubtful as to whether or not he could complete the path in this lifetime. He then asked the Grand Master, "Grand Master, in my next life…"

Before he could finish his question, the Grand Master immediately chided him, "Next life? Practice is that one thought extends to be an eon and an eon is in one thought. In this very lifetime, liberate yourself from the cycle of life and death."

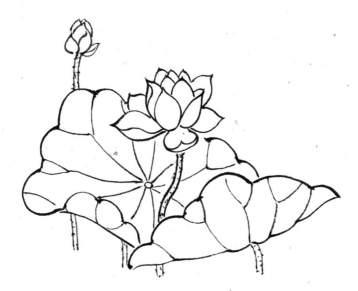

The Best Laid Plans

Before becoming a member of the Sangha, a certain monk's nickname was 'Perfect Planner.' On the night he was ordained, he immediately planned a schedule for practice: Every day he would recite the *Diamond Sutra* seven times, chant the Great Compassion mantra 108 times, prostrate to the Buddha 108 times...

After three days, the Grand Master asked him, "How do you feel after becoming a monk?" He replied proudly, "I chant the Great Compassion mantra 108 times every day," thinking that the Grand Master would be proud of his diligence. But instead the Grand Master replied, "Don't chant any mantra."

The monk thought, "If I do not chant any mantra, then it should be okay to recite sutras?" So he said to the Grand Master, "I also recite the *Diamond Sutra* seven times and do prostration 108 times everyday." The Grand Master said, "Don't recite any sutra and don't do prostration."

The monk was dumbfounded and finally asked, "Grand Master, if a monk doesn't recite sutras, doesn't do prostration, what should he do?" The Grand Master answered, "Keep the present mind still as such, and contemplate on the Middle Way Reality."

Is It Hot Inside?

During the hot season, to keep the computers functioning properly, the air-conditioning in the computer room at the Ling Chuan Monastery was always on. The monk in charge of the computer room worked so diligently to the point where he often neglected his meals and sleep. His dedication and sincerity had touched the Dharma Guardian, and one day a big Dharma wheel appeared on the cabinet in the computer room.

Some time later the monk sensed some annoyance raised in his mind. He remained in the computer room but he was bored. At that exact moment the Grand Master happened to pass by his window.
The Grand Master asked, "Is it hot inside?"
The monk answered, "Not hot."
The Grand Master asked again, "Is it hot inside?"
The monk answered again, "Not hot."

The monk felt strange, knowing that there was air-conditioning in the room, but why did the Grand Master ask him twice consecutively whether it was hot or not inside? After a while he began to understand, "the Grand Master must be referring to the hotness and annoyance in my mind." He suddenly thought of something and went to the cabinet. There he found that the Dharma wheel had disappeared.

Zhao Zhou's Cypress Tree

Once in a discussion session on the *Shurangama Sutra* at the Chung Tai Buddhist Institute, a monk brought up a famous Chinese koan.

> A monk asked Chan Master Zhao Zhou, "What is the essence of the Dharma?" The Chan Master replied, "The cypress tree in front of the court yard."

The disciple asked the Grand Master, "But Grand Master, I don't understand why the essence of the Dharma is the cypress tree in front of the court yard." Everyone held their breaths waiting…

The Grand Master firmly responded, "It indeed is the cypress tree in front of the court yard."

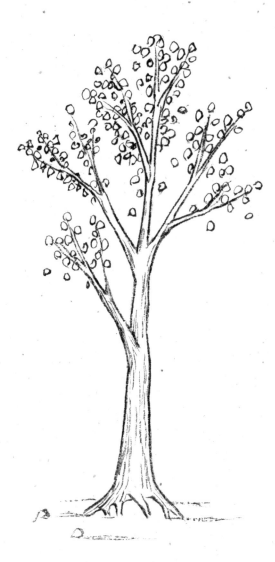

The Right Place

One day a lay disciple offered a very expensive tree to the monastery. The Grand Master handed it over to a monk and instructed, "Find a place to plant this tree." The very next morning, the Grand Master said, "This place is not good; plant the tree over there." The monk followed the Grand Master's instruction.

In the afternoon, the Grand Master interrogated him, "Who asked you to plant it here? Plant it in that place over there." Sweating, the monk dug up the tree and planted it again.

That same evening, the Grand Master again commanded him, "It is planted too far left; move it over a little to the right."

After the tree was given to the monastery, the monk stayed very busy planting it. He planted the tree in the morning, dug it out in the afternoon. Having planted it in the afternoon, he dug it out again in the evening. Having planted it one day, he dug it out the next day.

Observing the repetitive nature of the planting, a lay disciple felt pity and told the Grand Master, "The tree costs a lot. If we keep moving it around, will it not die?"

The Grand Master replied, "If it can help a disciple to grow mature and attain realization, however expensive the tree is, would it not be worth the price?"

Awakening or Realizing?

There was a monk who had been meditating for quite some time but seemingly could not find his way. One day, he asked the Grand Master, "What is the difference between the great awakening and realizing the Dharma body?"

The Grand Master replied, "To discover the difference, you must first gain the great awakening on your own!"

Grow Up Faster

A monk was assigned to an important post in the monastery; he felt that he was not competent for the job and explained to the Grand Master, "Master, I don't have any experience in this area. I am afraid that I would not do it well."

The Grand Master responded, "If you are elected to be the president, can you say, 'I have no experience?' You only acquire the experience after you have done it."

After sometime, the monk felt the responsibility was still too heavy and felt very much stressed. He made another request to the Master, "Grand Master, if a kid is wearing the shirt of an adult, it would be too loose; he is unable to support it." The Grand Master responded, "In that case, eat more and grow up faster!"

A Dilemma

In an official announcement, a monk was assigned to be the head of the Receptionist Office. The Grand Master instructed him, "In the reception room, there should be only monks or only nuns. Monks and nuns should not stay in one room." But, in the small receptionist office, besides him, all other receptionists were nuns.

From then on, the Grand Master always directed the chief receptionist monk, "Monks and nuns should not work together in one room. You are responsible for your own chores; you should be crystal clear with every matter."

The Grand Master counseled the monk many times with the same enigmatic directions. He was really puzzled and unable to retain a calm mind. Suddenly, he had a thought, "Grand Master could not really be scolding me. He was really just showing me the way."

When the Grand Master scolded him the next time, "Monks and nuns ..." The chief receptionist monk answered respectfully, "Yes!" No more troubling thoughts about this situation arose in his mind, and the Grand Master stopped scolding him.

Where Is the Dharma Wheel?

During the Little Stars Camp which lasted for two months, all of the monks, nuns, and lay disciples who volunteered in the camp were working diligently and sacrificing most of their sleeping and resting time. All of the activities were extremely wonderful, but during the camp there was no sign of the auspicious Dharma wheel. The monk in charge was puzzled, and he asked the Master, "Grand Master, why didn't the Dharma wheel ever appear during the Little Stars Camp?"

The Grand Master answered, "The Dharma wheel is in your eyes, in your smiles, and in your Dharma talks. How can you say that there isn't any Dharma wheel?" The monk did not comprehend the question and remained silent.

Some time later after the camp ended, the Grand Master was expounding on two statements in a discussion class, "True Dharma is concealed in the eyes," and "Pick up a flower and smile in return." The monk immediately understood the meaning of their previous conversation and smiled.

Pure Land Construction Awaits You

A monk had immigrated to the United States with his family in his youth. Even though he had studied Buddhism for many years and had intended to become a monk, he had never heard of the Grand Master Wei Chueh.

One night in his dream, he saw an old monk meditating on a huge stone. He moved forward and asked, "Is it true that the Pure Land is as magnificent as described in the sutras?" The old monk opened his eyes and spoke kindly, "The Pure Land has not been completed; its construction is awaiting you." When he heard this, he was very surprised and puzzled.

The next day, a friend invited him to attend a Dharma talk by the Grand Master who was visiting the United States. After listening to the illuminating and perfect talk of the Grand Master that pointed directly towards the nature of the mind, he was filled with joy in the Dharma. He thought, "Grand Master, if I have the opportunity to be a monk, please remember to call me." The Grand Master suddenly beckoned him from far away. He knew that he was going to become a monk.

One year after he became a monk, he had a chance to ask the Grand Master some questions regarding the Chan School and the Pure Land School. The Grand Master said, "Chan is the cause. Pure Land is the result. If we do not work hard on the cause, how can we have the result of Pure Land? Therefore, the Pure Land is not yet completed; it awaits you for its construction. "When the monk heard this, he was very surprised. He said to the Grand Master immediately, "I have dreamed of this before."

The Grand Master laughed and said, "Indeed! Dreams sometimes can tell us truth, too."

How Old Are You?

A group of visitors was visiting the monastery, and one of them asked curiously, "Grand Master, how old are you?" The Grand Master remained silent.

The visitor asked again for the second time, "Grand Master, how old are you?" And still the Master did not reply.

The visitor asked one more time very loudly, "Grand Master, I mean, how-old-are-you?"

The Grand Master asked him in return, "From which life time should I start the counting?"

Chung Tai Koans

The Grand Master's Smile

A monk was joyously reporting his meditation experience in the Abbot Office. The Grand Master looked at him, smiled, and did not say anything. After a few days, this monk was annoyed by something; he came again to the Abbot Office to talk about his difficulty. The Grand Master was still looking at him, smiled, and did not say a word.

The monk looked at the Grand Master's smile that was so familiar to him and reminded him of the distinctly different state of mind he had a few days ago. For him, the Grand Master's smile seemed to be saying, "Not moved in the stillness is not the real stability, not moved in the motion is the true stability."

Thundering

One day when the Grand Master was giving a Dharma talk to the public, a lay disciple who sat behind the Grand Master had many wandering thoughts. He even consoled himself thinking, "That's okay. The Grand Master does not know what I am thinking."

Unexpectedly, the Grand Master abruptly stopped his talk and turned his head to look at the lay disciple saying, "The thoughts of ordinary people are as loud as the sound of thunder."

Supernatural Revelations

Ordinary people usually view supernatural power with a sense of awe and mystery. One day, a lay disciple came to the monastery. Seeing the Grand Master, he asked immediately, "Grand Master, do you have supernatural power?" The Master smiled and did not respond to the question.

After a little while, the disciple asked again, "Do you really have supernatural power?" In this way, he asked the same question repeatedly.

Suddenly the Grand Master turned to his side, asking him softly, "You have a deposit of a few million dollars in your savings account. Do you want to tell others about it?" After hearing this, the lay disciple was silent.

Reality Check

A disciple said, "Grand Master, I really, really want to change my chores!" The Grand Master replied, "In this world there is nothing real."

Unordinary in the Ordinary

In a meeting to prepare for setting up a meditation center, a monk was sitting next to the Grand Master and started to examine the Grand Master's face carefully. He thought in his mind, "The face of the Grand Master is full of wrinkles, and from that he is no different from any ordinary old man. Then why are these prestigious people so respectful of him?"

After the meeting, when all the lay disciples had left, the Grand Master talked to the monks and nuns, "No conceptual thought in the awareness; awareness is without attachment. When, through practice, one has attained a very high level, in outward appearance he or she will look just like any other ordinary person, but his or her mind will be totally different. This is what we call *covering the illumination and being in harmony with the ordinary.*"

Chung Tai Chan Monastery and Affiliates Outside Taiwan

Chung Tai Chan Monastery
1 Chung Tai Road, Puli
Nantou, Taiwan, ROC
Tel (049) 2930-215
Fax (049) 2930-397
www.CTworld.org

Chung Tai Zen Center of Houston
12129 Bellaire Boulevard
Houston, TX 77072
Tel 281.568.1568
Fax 281.568.1569
www.CTHouston.org
email: Zen@CTHouston.org

Buddha Gate Monastery
3254 Gloria Terrace
Lafayette, CA 94549
Tel 925.934.2411
Fax 925.934.2911
www.BuddhaGate.org

Chung Tai Zen Center
of Los Angeles
20836 Marcon Drive
Walnut, CA 91789
Tel 909.595.7313
Fax 909.598.1128

Chung Tai Zen Center of
Sunnyvale
1031 N. Fair Oaks Avenue
Sunnyvale, CA 94089
Tel 408.747.1099
Fax 408.747.1098
www.ctzen.org
email: sunnyvale@ctzen.org

Chung Tai Chan Monastery USA
12129 Bellaire Boulevard
Houston, TX 77072
Tel 281.568.1568
Fax 281.568.1569
www.CTHouston.org

Buddha Mind Temple
5916 S. Anderson Road
Oklahoma City, OK 73150

Ocean Sky Chan Monastery
716 Jose Abad Santos St.
Little Baguio, San Juan,
Metro Manila, Philippines
Tel 632.723.6132
Fax 632.722.4400

PuGuang Meditation Center
G/F, No. 7 Moreton Terrace,
Causeway Bay, Hong Kong
Tel 852.2915.6011
Fax 852.2915.6700

Great Buddha Monastery
61/84~86 Mooban Thaveemit,
Rama 9 Road
Bangkok 10320 Thailand
Tel (66) 264.32386
Fax (66) 264.32795

Glossary

Amitabha
Chinese translation is Amitofo. The most commonly used name for the Buddha of Infinite Light and Infinite Life. A transhistorical Buddha venerated by all Mahayana schools, particularly, Pure Land. In the Pure Land School of Buddhism, Amitabha presides over the Western Pure Land (Land of Ultimate Bliss) where anyone can be reborn through single minded faith in him.

Amitofo
See Amitabha.

Awakening
See enlightenment.

Bhiksu/Bhiksuni
A fully ordained monk of the Buddhist sangha. Feminine: Bhiksuni is a fully ordained Buddhist nun. Sometimes bhikshu/bhikshuni.

Bodhidharma
The Twenty-Eighth Patriarch who came from India bringing the Chan Teachings to China in 520 A.D., also known as the First Chinese Chan or Zen Patriarch.

Bodhisattva
One who aspires to the attainment of Buddhahood and devotes oneself to altruistic deeds, especially deeds that cause others to attain enlightenment.

Buddha
Awakened One. One who has attained Perfect Enlightenment. Particularly applies to Siddhartha Gautama, also known as *Shakyamuni Buddha*, the founder of Buddhism.

Buddha nature
Is the true, immutable, and ever-present nature of all sentient beings. Mahayana Buddhism generally holds that all sentient beings have Buddha nature and therefore have the innate potential to realize Buddhahood.

Chan (Ch'an)
The school of Mahayana Buddhism in China founded by Bodhidharma (6th century). In Chan, enlightenment is attained by seeing one's true nature through the direct perception of one's own mind with the practice of meditation. The word Chan predates the Japanese word Zen. Chan Buddhism originated in China and then came to Japan where it became known as Zen Buddhism and was later popularized by the same name in Western cultures.

Dharma
All phenomena, and also, the teachings of the Buddha.

Dharma Wheel
Symbolizes the teaching of a Buddha. It is like the wheel that crushes all illusions.

Dhyana
See meditation.

Enlightenment
An individual's awakening to the mind's true nature. A state of perfect wisdom and limitless compassion. The achievement of a Buddha or the state of Buddhahood.

Hui Neng
The sixth Chinese Chan Patriarch and the most influential, he was the founder of the Southern School of Chan or Zen, which emphasized sudden enlightenment. All current Chan lineages trace back to Hui Neng.

Karma
Root meaning *action*. Derived meaning, action, and the appropriate result of action. The Buddhist doctrine of cause and effect; the law of causality. The effect of an action taken today, whether good or bad, may come to manifest many years from now or even in a subsequent lifetime. No actions are isolated and independent; all are tied together in cause and effect.

Mahakasyapa

The Chan School of Buddhism regarded him as their First Patriarch from the story of the 'transmission of the mind seal' when Buddha held up a golden flower and Mahakasyapa smiled.

Maitreya

The Buddha to come. The bodhisattva who will be the next Buddha and currently said to reside in Tusita Heaven or one of the heavens.

Meditation

Also known as *dhyana* and is one of the three major components of the Buddhist way along with *morality* (or precept-keeping which precedes and must always accompany the activity of meditation), and *wisdom*, which is achieved as a result of meditation. In Buddhism, meditation is an activity where one is engaged in both subduing discursive thought, destroying or discouraging unwholesome mental states, and initiating or nourishing wholesome mental states. This discipline must be learned from a master. Without such personal supervision, it cannot be properly undertaken. One of the principal reasons for the existence of the Buddhist monastery is as a school of meditation where new monks learn from more advanced monks.

Nirvana

Ultimate goal of Buddhist endeavor is the permanent cessation of all suffering; release from the limitations of existence. State of being forever freed from all delusions and suffering, and realizing ultimate tranquility and bliss.

Patriarch

In Buddhism, title of the founder of a school or his designated successor in the transmission of its teachings.

Samadhi

Profound meditative state; a very deep concentrated state of mind.

Samsara
World of rebirth and death. The cycle of birth and death and suffering of ordinary sentient beings.

Sangha
The community of ordained Buddhist monks and nuns. Sometimes referring to the community of ordained and lay practitioners as a whole.

Sentient Beings
All beings that experience pain and suffering.

Shifu
Chinese translation means Dharma Master. It is one way to address a Buddhist monk or nun.

Sutra
Generally scriptures. The canon containing the dialogues and discourses of the Buddha.

Three Jewels
See triple gem.

Three Refuges
To take the Three Refuges under a Dharma Master is to formally become a Buddhist and to begin the path of enlightenment. By taking the Three Refuges, one also formalizes one's commitment to the Triple Gem.

Triple Gem
The fundamental constituents of Buddhism: The Buddha, the Dharma, and the Sangha, also known as the Three Jewels.